REA

7.19.78

Planet of Winds

By the same author

The Charted Mirror: Literary and Critical Essays
The Landfallers: a Poem in Twelve Parts
The Story of the Night: Studies in Shakespeare's Major
                              Tragedies
Wood and Windfall
Later English Broadside Ballads (edited with Joan Black)
The Proud Knowledge

Planet of Winds

Poems by

John Holloway

Routledge & Kegan Paul

London, Henley and Boston

First published in 1977
by Routledge & Kegan Paul Ltd
39 Store Street,
London WC1E   7DD,
Reading Road,
Henley-on-Thames,
Oxon RG9 1EN and
9 Park Street,
Boston, Mass. 02108, USA
Set in IBM Century
and printed in Great Britain by
Lowe & Brydone Printers Limited, Thetford, Norfolk
© this collection John Holloway 1977

ISBN   0 7100 8515 X

Contents

Acknowledgments

Acknowledgment is gratefully made to: *Art International,*
The Cambridge Review, Country Life, The Critical Quarterly,
English, Esquire, The Hudson Review, The Malahat Review,
New Poetry I, Outposts, Solstice, Stand, The Times Literary
Supplement, **and** *Wave,* in which some of these poems have
already been published.

A Poem for Breakfast

Look!
We have a great frost.   An
Arrival of north.
And in the blue dark and bed,
Feeling it, I edged nearer and
You were southern.

Sparrows
Are the gay birds.   We have them
Queuing at the fronded panes
And we all share chatter and bread.
But they have
No use for your beautiful
Coffee.

Cold, and well,
Yes, grief, are so alike, the
Wise man does not stay
To feel either but
Edges south to such
Climates as you
Magically provide;   and
Look!   Now we have the Land of Talk.

Yet, wisewoman, consider also
The nature of magic:
Which resides
Also in the so
Happily, so hungrily
Enchanted. Therefore
Replenish my cup: from your
Shapely vessel and other
Morning abundances.

An Evening Poem

Time to prepare for
The felicitous hour
That shall bring an end of
Uncleanness

Of the spirit also ... in
What is plain and evident like
Going to bed:
All goodness, while

Energies enough to
Spin planet like a pebble
Bury in brightness
Diminishing

As this wind turns breeze
And that calm, and we
Close our books
Undress

And as stars bring brightness back we
Are lustral. Fit to share
This knowledge of cleanness, this
Of darkness.

3

Stars in the House

Stars in the house! They waterfall the stairs
From the big window. Rain has sweetened
The air into clearness.
At the stairfoot
Silence. The doorways
Leading through to more windows and gold
And they mill by
Millions. After
A great journey, light
Gathers, it is inside us.

Wind kindled this. Scoured us
Ocean-clean. Great currents have
Galed us. This night
Deep in an eastern inland, still
We are drenched to mine-level,
To the water-table. Wind's other harvest,
Rain gone to ground,
Speeds at the black arches and
For this the bright
Herring, dark
Porpoise shall veer in the
Mile-wide currents, and whalefood
Star salt water.

If I get my choice let it be
Such flood and such burning. Distanced
Into flow or starwork. A moment
Of seeding in a radiant –
Better! A creative darkness.

Lunar Moment

Before us, a weathered stone
   and a light leaf
rest side by side
   on the earth, do

you take up the heavy
   and I take up the light and
if our eyes meet
   under this high moon, let it

come with a gaze of such
   knowledge as lies in fingers
that can hold such things
   for a moment or more

with proprietorship
   eloquent in a touch.
you are cold with frost.
   the breath once out of your lips

could be some kind of ghost.
   so how can the rest of you
be a good smiling beast
   with something tall and strange

I can hardly give a name to?
   now what you hold is warm.
now night air stirs my leaf.
   come in out of this moon.

Morning Star

dear killer, dear thief
        (of boredom, of blankets) I watch you with
the sun on your strong head, stony
        with sleep, but refreshing into morning
with a gentle breath. your eyes

so that you do not know
        theft of wind on pear-orchard
in a swirl of petals
        that snowily scale the window.
shadows flicker on a woman

staunch with sleep. but mortal. some
        killer of a morning, that is,
shall blow you, with petals,
        to sleep, one day, about the sun
for a long time and all the same

we may number it in minutes. make me, therefore,
        hard for gentleness, in what time
we have, and the facts of the case,
        killer of boredom, thief of the morning
star asleep in the sun.

Fruit Poem

Star or frost
    where they
        have cupped themselves
or suddenly flutter to the earth:
        spent

white petals
    that fall
        on the path
having been floriated once and
        empty now

of weight or promise
    because
        promise has gone
into the rain-washed stubs that
        will make apples as

I ask myself
    what promise
        is left now
still on the tree, or star fruit
        before frost and

answer from the sky
    wind
        rising
night and petals fall, and rain –
        rain washing.

8

First Chill

A town on a hill.
As you go down, away
From the great church, to the great
Plains in the sun, they lie before you
Sheeted with sky, sheeted with wind,
Enormous with morning: and flashed,
Flashed with fruition of the grain.

We cannot manage it.
It will be the death of us.
Terror is all around us, in the light
Sharper than in darkness.

Buttresses and pinnacles
Are grey, if you look back,
With a greyness at least of distance
Across miles of the harvested and

A little town on a hill
Smudged under its church. A great
Gravestone on a skyline
Among terror of wind, of sky
And miles of ripening

Which is the sun, buried
Until we feed, and sustain life

But we cannot manage it.
On these murderous mornings, an old man
Walking with a dog.

Sheeted with wind, cold
In the burying sun,
The earth is patient
As you go down to it.

Mire Poem

... and even if radiances are falling, to dissolve
      formlessly as rain:
sheetings and flashings that become, with nightfall
      melting

anonymous, muddy ... the boot
      to plod with a thud
over fallow, by the bored hare, there is still
      brilliance,

truthfully, its dazzle, a cloudscape
      integral and enormous
of cirrus above nimbus, withdrawn from the walker
      to where angels

have clouded, I suppose, and occluded, into matter
      for the eye: how else
might upper air, sited above nightfall,
      so dramatize

that empire of light, remembered roseately
      now, from journeys in
aircraft, on this journey: the trudged track
      where snipe

and redshank, from mired sedge
      or cat-ice, flush
heavenward: twistings and evadings they need not
      rebuke me with,

nor will their blood-bought upsurge
    into darkness, take them
near that wheel of light, circling the earth
    now starrily.

Twice a Blue Moon

Is it once, is it twice a blue moon
A *Radical* turns out a *Rat?*
Till you'd sooner have the whole bench of Bishops.
Still the hairiest rat in the Circus
Is a rat that can talk:
So call in the odd sod and bobtail
And we'll have some discussion.
A participate-in, one and all;
You go for the needles and vodka,
I'll turn the clock-face to the wall.

Here's all my friends, and my country
Tumbling from rich down to poor
Till at just about three o'clock in the weather
There's a knock at the door
And you needn't suppose it's the postman
Or father come back from the dead,
There's no coming back for the wicked
Since there's just none at all,
Which is something to put in your pocket.

Once Jonathan Swift on his horse
Rode the strand with his groom and his dog.
Next he walked all day long in his house.
Next he sat in his chair like a log.
'A hundred and twenty fine poets'
(The finest that ever were seen)
'Of every sex and condition'
Were reddening the right ear of Sir Robert Walpole.
I Am What I Am said the Dean.

13

The poets' obsession is sex.
Yes yes it's a very fine thing.
If you've got it like leaves on the tree
Your bed is perpetual spring ...
Yet to always play toot on the horn,
The Queen of the Night may be Hecate
(Which puts a new light, you see, on copulation)
But I think there's a groove in your record,
The needle yes needle seems stuck.

They do it for thousands of dollars,
My my how the campuses ring
(Let's breathe it by phrases now shall us?)
Their typewriters tip-tap and ting:
No Sir, it's the Holy Rollers have people rolling in the aisles
The Writing School's over this summer,
So hitch-hike to Paris in France
O Captain my Captain:
Or pull the chain, sink with the *Ship*.

You can transplant new hearts now for lovers,
But it's love that grows old I can show
By the lines in the palms of my gloves,
Or you'll find it in La Rochefoucauld
Written out, black and white, in his *Maxims;*
And when love grows old, it's quite plain
There's nothing but Stuff-up-your-Jacksie
And should you want the Jackpot and Golden Handshake
Show me a man not afraid.

14

What we did to O'Connells, Macdonalds,
It's stored in a warm egg for us:
The Russians are bringing their reaper
And it isn't part of any Agricultural Exchange Programme.
Should they get to old age like the rest,
My small son and hay-headed daughter –
No fear of a terminal illness
Except if they follow the Mayflower ...
But That Is one.

Truth used to be plain as plain day,
And sweet as the rose.
Sam. Johnson, the stone in his way
He booted it straight into Berkeley:
But now I snort out through my nose
At genuine straight or sincere
Things have got so untidy;
And they're still singing *hen wlad fy nhadau**
For LBJ ... or it could be President Whiskers.

The Poker School's over my son.
Every card is a Joker.
So blow out the candle and run.
I can't bring my thoughts to a focus.
I really can't tell which is which
Any more, not from first-born to bastard.
But if all of us die in a ditch
Isn't that where we started,
Howling, and rosy with blood?
Or is it where all the flowers bud?

15

*Hen wlad fy nhadau is the Welsh national anthem:
'(Old) Land of my fathers'

Turn

In this terrible time, when all
likenesses are let-downs (no
birds soar now, they stumble; grimed
snowfalls foul fountains; garlands
     grow gnarled) do you

regain empty idea. denude
analogy by a nude
resolve pent in the pen's
hard moving to be grim
     for excellence. this

growth alone knows
the end of: but that
shows in fulness, perhaps
an honest stroke of the hand, such
     as is primary to primates

and the part of speech we can
(unfashionable fact) pare into
the parent, transparent if right,
of fully to know what is: index
     indicating the human.

The Total Dance

Come by the hand into the Narrow House.
Take the rings from your finger, the gold out of
   your mouth,
And put the flesh to use.
And I will put the bones. Now come the General
   Pause.
The ring is hollow on the stone floor. Come forth
Into the last light, look at the doors
That open on to no mortal pain.
A dusky night rides down the sky. Dance, because
Here is the Narrow House and what the House
   contains.

Listen! - Now I strike the note! I strike
Total and Dominus into a sudden sun.
Come little fish, set to the pike,
Adam and Children of Adam, Adam and his wife,
Join the Serpent where the dancing has begun
Livelier than how you ever danced in your life.
Bubo bubo bubo, I hear the ambulance:
No need for psycho- or physiotherapy if
You follow. Here's a prisoner I have got, so dance.

It's Fusion time Miss Model, the Four shall make
   One, and all
The pushers, whores and Ministers lie sprawled
   across the floor,
The song shall turn to a howl on the other side of the
   Wall,

So look, Mr Consultant, in the belly of the Fish,
If that's how the betting lies, I will go one more,
Till Jill shall have her Jack, every Jack his wish,
And one morning you shall find Me grinning at your
    side,
And every Ready Reckoner shall sup the same dish:
Below the waist the Fiend's, and above the Neck,
    Void.

Brother Fox has a Full House, but Mr Hedgehog
    leads Ace,
And all the little foxes that monkey with the vines
Shall soil the cities and fire the Holy Places.
Brother Knife shall pair you, depend on Brother Hook,
Brother Fork shall dance you, up along his tines;
So wash your hands Lord Chamberlain, you're in the
    Book,
And my two tall servants, their names are Letch and
    Itch,
Skip first for them, then for Me; and whichever way
    you look,
Madness and Civilisation, you tell me which is which.

Mister Major General, lock away your sabre
And your snow-white epaulettes, coal-black plumes,
    cockade.
Opt for *pas-de-deux,* join me in a caper
And if that's where the footfall - I will go one more,
Show a leg Professor, proffer my trade now,

Vade mecum, down the total dancing floor;
He'll allow no saving today, the saviour of the Fiery
　　Eye,
Once you're *ex cathedra,* knock a locked door,
Black Bull shall fight Red Bull, and stars fall from
　　the sky.

You can grovel in the grey sea for gas, be slick for
　　oil,
Think wealth is water, you'll be gravelled for a groat
The day such a groundswell comes as makes the
　　water steam and boil:
Captains, and Commodores, shall rout on the fog-
　　horn
Or hornpipe up the mainmast, that shan't save the
　　boat;
Red sky at evening shall last till stormy dawn,
And the scorch of noon and evening burn up all
　　　Lovely Homes
Till better to die than live, and best be not born,
And when I win the rubber, all reverts to bones.

Tucket and sennet for trumpet, never one so loud:
The First Angel shall plummet out of a blue sky
And the Second Angel shall plummet out of that
　　fountaining cloud
And I will go One More: the Last Angel to show
Shall come out of a Black Hole in space and make the
　　babies cry.

By Watergate and dustcart, whichever way you go
Peine forte et dure, says Anthropophagos.
What she set her heart on is what she must forego:
We lost the Flower of England, what more had we to
    lose?

You stand among the Needy, I do not speak in pride:
Some stand there early morning, some not till
    afternoon,
But what does not change has seen you, so the
    bidding's your side;
Old Burno the Man-in-the-Moon, the burn's life-
    critical now,
Shall burn his sticks in a Fire, under a Blood-red
    Moon:
I put my Bone to my Fiddle, the way I know how,
It roars like a great engine, it roars like a great
    bomb,
The Sun can burst and scatter to the Seven Stars in
    the Plough,
But you'll not need any light any more, from here to
    Kingdom Come.

Songs

The due prize. A question
of the late hour.
This is my fear.
I say, let it be:
but he will not.

At twilight, over grey river,
that gooseskein flushed
to a sunburn like blood:
ground in darkness with
sky in darkness with
geese winging starwise where

East Coast runs
ragstone and weatherbed to
holy islands; and oil; and seals we
cull (language, the due
prize) as we do flowers, killing
mother and child. Put
your trust in nothing, seals,
as you sing for me

good woman,
have you heard them also
calling mate, across the grey, red
belaboured water? My
belief is we do not
match them in music, nor
(which is my fear)
in mating. Let it be.

Put your trust
in nothing. Yet, on this road,
and in the dark,
a man laboured at my car. His
heartfed hands
glinted grey, oil. He hummed
and grunted: 'I'd as soon be at work'.
Let it be, good man,
the due prize ... which is my fear
this bloodred time.

Stealers

My apple-twig pile, ringed,
Robbed, with a nibble, shows
The wet white of the wood
To heart-height all round.
Teeth. Bud and red bark-strand
Melted in moonlight for food.

Food! Now I am up to
Those dwarf hedge-gaps, and what
The moon lures from the forest
To prize them, gently. What,
Before the sun, draw back
Into pools, wells of shadow.
Wood-fed creatures.

Creatures! - so to come and do,
Like them, with lightness. Returning
To an earlier thing. Dark then
Of sheet and pillow (as deer
Steal around the house) be my
Apple-sweet feeding.

The Birds are
Shooting the Moon

Below, broad mortal dolls-house.
Above, bright bird-light cirrus.
    Through cold we wing
    And song all sing
With only star-shine near us.
Dark air burns up with swordplay.
Sharp wind black season hacks us.
    What should birds know
    As south they go
Of Earth on leaning axis?

Below, dull dolls world distance.
New raw roads rip ripe autumn.
    We fly past Kent
    Sark Brest Ushant,
Grey seas see great ships dawdle.
Our friends, they were of the poorest,
But they drove us from green poison:
    Old rust-red can
    Red Rag-Bag Man
Wave to us in the wind rejoicing.

Down through the golden forests,
Generalissimo-handsome,
    Big pheasants strut
    From butt to butt
Each breathless breast spreads crimson.
Mars and the Moon admonish us
To fly and never to falter,
    Up down we're tossed

At our backs frost
Before we reach Gibraltar.

Mere wings make all bird wisdom.
So bird-wit-wise we reckon.
    Add three to four
    That makes two score,
Twice two, that comes out seven.
And yet black's black, white's whiter.
Cold come close made us anxious.
    But far down below
    Where great lights glow
Glows one great *ignis fatuus.*

Earth rind lies thin men burn it.
We race down airy rivers.
    North Pole is friend
    Strong wind he'll send
To fling bird on like feathers.
Gold in the Bank of England
Stone dead though spreads with standing:
    Sun weightless gold
    Remote from cold
Waits where we look for landing.

Bald songless wingless humans
Crowd like gnats big millions;
    Yet only walk
    And talk talk talk,

How shall they last long winters?
Feathers, smooth wings win fleeing.
Our dry feet hot with radar
    Even now
    We pass by the Plough
Seven Stars and Drunken Sailor.

The Hunter towers above us
And we have the Poor Man's Answer:
    But if that's *No,*
    We still flee snow,
The Moon's our Nightly Dancer.
Due south, beyond the Pillars
Of Hercules we wander
    And halt our flight
    When dawn grows bright
And climb down Jacob's Ladder.

Sun spring up ball and bonfire,
Red ring quit morning's margin;
    Red spark by spark
    We drop from dark
See toy trees speed up larger.
Tired wing fold find finale,
Heat south still spring-time weather,
    From sky fall deep
    All fall asleep
Black day dark snow soft feather.

First Light

Morning Glory!—the first cock crowing
    To rip the night red with *Morning Glory!*
    Splashing on the starry sky with that story
And never a faggot of daylight showing

Yet but *Solfatara!* across the darkness
    Of the star-drenched sky, the rock-drenched mountain
    Where you hear *Solfatara!* erupt, fountain,
Drench across a world still asleep, still in darkness

Till *Come Along Sun!* one fires at the dawning
    Fire in the east and Orion faded
    Over stone-locked vineyards still heavy-shaded
Ringing *Come Along Sun!* to a lighting-up morning

But *Nothing Left to Eat!*—now two or three are screaming
    Morning Glory! or *Solfatara!*
    Or *Come Along Sun!* all the cocks tantarara
And one that stabs me out of my dreaming

With *Nothing Left...* and I hear it add... *To Eat*
    From the bleak brown stone-yard the sun just flashed on
    From the black-blue sky a cock has just gashed on
With what the island echoes to: *Nothing Left to Eat!*

Just a Gay Tipple for Twelfth Night

The rats in the loft are alive.
    I hear them all night at their song.
They sing in two parts three four five.
    Then they ring their alarm-bells ding dong
Because cats in the cellars belt up -
                Ho Ho!
Black, tortoise-shell, tabby - there's dozens.
    If they plan to eat next up above
It's not because rats are cats' cousins -
                No No!
    It's hunger yes hunger say love.

The rats hear the cats on the stairs -
                Tramp Tramp!
    Each thrills at the other's aroma.
They're dancing they're screaming in pairs.
    I hide in my lounge with my Homer.
(He hides in his lounge with his girl:
    His sofa's resilient Bounce Bounce!)
And as Pussy wants In for the Kill,
    As Pussy's preparing to pounce,
We learn all about heroes we thrill.

My daughter has ears like a mouse,
    Late at night she can hear the oak beams
Gently manoeuvre our house
    To the gentle south wind or the snow-laden streams tha
Flame icily down from the Pole.
    The moon's very brilliant tonight.
I drive like a cat now I'm old.

The woods all spread lunar dead white.
I'll be late for the children blast blast.

These trees are all paper just look.
  Write poems by dozens dear scribe!
These bare trees drum rattle knock knock.
  But once it was warmer Inside ...
Remember? We spread out the *Times,*
  Four copies, and quick we lay down.
I went back when the oaks were dead brown.
  Then again. They were tinsel with rime.
And nothing was there but the pulp
  Where we'd made the hill warm with our cold.

In those snow-laden woods, branches snap.
  Our riches have made us mouse-poor.
It's time now to whisker the trap.
  There's no bacon-rind lying about any more,
'O Solitude where are the charms ...?'
  (Dear Cowper, two hares and no gun -
                            Bang Bang!.)
My own love will you starve in my arms?
  No my daughter must starve, or my son.

There's a butterfly trapped in my pane ...
  I shift up the sash and then blow.
Down the garden it soars off again.
  As I type I can still see it go -
                            Flap Flap!

... I ought to have left things alone.
    Snow's hell to that tortoise-shell spark.
My old dusty curtains were home:
    Its dear old familiar B-sharp
- If you fancy the new-fangle name.

Oak logs, wine for dinner, tip top.
    I bought the whole thing out of words.
My first work-room just a bare loft.
    - Now it's all faintly absurd.
What fifty-foot Cat with his Cutlass
    Strides in where I posted no sentry?
Let me take a quick look at the atlas
    And think about multiple nuclear re-entry
            Bang Bang!

Pack quick start the car we've an hour.
    Could we get into Wales before dawn?
High the peaks are, the valleys drop sheer.
    I can hear Roland's late absurd horn -
            Tromp Tromp!
But there's nowhere to go any more.
    What's a gesture but simply bounce bounce?
O my love O my dear love look here:
    We thought it was opening-time once,
Now it's closing time on the Fixed Star.
    Once we thought the day long now we don't.

Rules of Play

Take up your hand, and leave me mine.
If yours is kings and aces, so.
What cards make a true player repine?
Or if I repine, you're not to know.
Take up your own, and leave me mine.

My stars, you think, must be malign?
For you the zephyr, me the squall
Threatened in sextile, quart and trine?
All nights must wane, all bright stars fall.
Take up your own, and leave me mine.

Now if the Muses, one or nine,
Intrude upon our evening here
And into our two women combine,
Let yours be the beauty, mine's my dear:
Take up your own, and leave me mine.

Let's make a night of it? Why, fine ...
But let me tell you frankly how:
Let each man keep to his own wine.
My glass is full, I filled it now:
Take up your own, and leave me mine.

Let it taste gall, let it taste brine,
I cast one jewel into the can
Of finest water, and true sign
Making a man into a man: -
Take up your own, and leave me mine.

A Problem

Some have many, some have none,
Small may have great and great have small
And many have few. And I have One.
Tell me, computer science, the way to
Count one as All and More than All.
  – You can't.

Sevenfold seven in sevenfold prism
From Barbara right through to Baralipton –
Firework of sorites and syllogism –
Tell me, propositional logic, the way for
One to make All and All make One.
  – You don't know.

Social studies, please tell my why
All the people are dropping like flies
Into the bars as I make a call
From the red box at the end of the street;
And telephone directory give me the One
Number and only One the sweet
Music of the bell shall turn into All ...
  – There it is!

Up the steps I run and I rap on the door.
Propositional logic hides in the wall
And computer science gets under the floor
But the room's not empty, no not at all;
Personal Relation, tell me true
How One can be Some One All and More ? ?
  – Look!

Inch by Inch

Equity equally with lynch
Law, or courage - Dutch, French -
Has its characteristic stench:
Yes, *cum grano,* just a pinch:
     All comes down to inch by inch.

Gross as eagle, spick as finch
Dais, dispatch box, soap-box, bench,
After sunshine comes drench,
After sparring comes the clinch.
     Write its name down: inch by inch.

All drawn earthward as by winch
(Gradual pull or sudden wrench)
'All find safety' in the trench?
Those who think so, need not flinch??
     Let them learn, learn inch by inch.

Funeral Service

The she-cat my tom-cat admires
    Ran across to the clergyman's wife;
She bent down, stroked it, enquired
    Gently, why its voice was like a knife
And it kept on scraping at her foot.
    Then, thinking something amiss,
Bundled into her coat
    And across to the old fellow's house;
    But the old fellow's still fast asleep.
        And doesn't wake.

Dr Longlegs walks over quite quick
    (It's his long stride that makes it look slow)
But you hardly needed to look:
    Eighty-six, a fair time to go ...
        Burr-burr, burr-burr ...
Two spits deep he'd just dug his garden;
    He'd a light, airy swing with the spade;
That soil, like tea-leaves well sodden,
    Rich, dark, spring-like it lay
... Then the ambulance, clean as fresh cream:
    Dee-dah-dee-dah-dee-dah!
        - The old man's still asleep.

Now they've got him screwed down in that box.
    He's staring straight up through those flowers.
But those great bushy eye-brows, they're fixed.
    How he'd talk by the hour!
This time it's parson talking.

The trumpet shall sound
O Death where's thy sting?
   It's just six feet long, in the ground.
Dong ... Long ... Long ...
   'At Rest': so he's still not awake.

When they come to the grave ...
   My God but the wind cuts this March!
Man's cut down like a flower...
   The mute screws his fingers round archly:
He's forgotten his sand,
   And the ground's far too muddy
To dirty his hand with the planet:
   Earth to earth, dust to dust, crumble crumble.

It's the end of them all in the end.
   The old man didn't have
(So I hear) one kinsman or friend
   To freeze at the side of the grave.
Yet he needn't complain of his luck
   (Who alive can complain of his own?)
And in fact, they do say the old buck ...
   But then! If the truth were quite known
   Who'd get flowers?
Ting! Thank you ... Cold this morning.

Holstein, Riss, Eemian, Würm ...
   I think of Ice Ages. I think,
Twelve summers without any warm,

From the Severn across to the Trent
Would be Ice-front again ... I half run
    From my gate ... There's a flake on my coat.
That she-cat's gone stray.
    The wind's like ice. I'm not young
Any more - that's a nice way to say
    They May Want You Tonight.
Longlegs, burr-burr, fresh creamy van,
    Dee-dah-dee-dah! Long ... long
        Crumble crumble
        In pacem.

At the Hospital

You're ill and they can't get you right.
    I call with these flowers every day.
I ask Sister how you react.
    But I simply can't hear what she says.
There's something that nobody knows.
    It's in you it's in you it's in you.
When you lay in my hand like a rose
    It must have been there.
And I fancied I knew all there was.

So far as they think, you're a Bed.
    It's wonderful how things come round.
The very best woman I've had
    Can't put her foot to the ground.
How little I thought I should mind:
    Now I don't much like the look of it.
That whisky I managed to find,
    I noticed how little you took of it.
What demon has got in instead?

I talk to myself down the street.
    Reality rears like a flower ...
Squeal of brakes and a shout. I'm asleep.
    No, sleeping's what I was before,
When you were awake for the pair,
    And swallowing down life like a tot –
No we both did; and now there you are.
    They simply can't tell what you've got.
I'm a coward to see you look brave.

That clumsy great nurse with that Thing,
        She was pricking you, pricking for blood;
I could strangle her just with one hand
        When I think of that tube going red:
- Dear Nurse, no! *She* owes you *my* life:
        Or that's what it feels like out here
As I wait for the big clock to strike
        And She reaches down - I can't see,
But the pebbles themselves come alive.

'Are you frightened?' I'd asked as we lay
        Like peas, and 'What of?' was the answer
I watched her rehearse as she spoke,
        And with it, some kind of a glance
That made me start counting. Time's short,
        And I can't bear to count though I've tried.
So I stare at these flowers that I've brought:
        But the one I want's bedded inside.
Let me in this great glasshouse!   It's there.

The Night Out

You didn't do right what you did.
Was it you to be clumsy like that?
Sharp, sudden, those tears that you shed
As you just wanted out like the cat
And stood with your face to the door
Though you hadn't your coat, or your hat;
So I held it to let you walk out;
Aren't such things as that what men are for?
- Outside, very dark, bloody dark.

That night as I lay on that bed,
And the cold shuttered down like a knife,
In the treetop outside overhead
I heard Mr Owl and his wife
Hooting melodious music
Ninety foot up from the ground;
He called, and she called him as well ...
But I dreamed that those trees were sawn down,
And the sawing turned into that bell
That spurts like a flame from the clock.

Those homeless, those wingless at night,
Must walk all the way to the morning;
But don't seek it north west or south,
Nor east, nor below nor above you;
You closed it inside like a nut,
When you spoke it flew out of your mouth;
If you ask why I loved you
What reason had I more than that,

Nut Woman, large half of the World?
- It was harvest to have you.

Harold Wilson's dark mornings again:
I sit with my coffee and egg;
There must be some salt, we've mislaid;
You didn't do right, what you did;
No you didn't you didn't you didn't;
But the slam of the gate in its catch
And the rustle (I hear it like silk)
Of footsteps that run on my path
- That's the milk? Just the milk? Yes, it's milk.

The Mirror

A poet and his coloured girl,
Out walking, find this silent park.
A poet and his coloured girl
Find this great house, quiet in the sun,
Empty; find the wrought latch undone,
Explore the cool, quiet, high half-dark.

Hand in hand, from room to room,
They stroll, admiring as they pass,
Frieze, architrave and tympanum
That frame them in. Now, from the wall,
Great lights let squares of great light fall.
And here - the old, foxed cheval-glass

Behind a pool of sunshine, stands
Still as a stone to mark a grave.
Silvered once by some craftsman's hands
In a quiet English market town,
The glass rests firmly in the brown
Mahogany, planked once by some slave.

Looking, they see themselves. And then,
In the inter-locking glass and frame,
See themselves, much more linked, again.
Half-troubled, half defiant, half sure,
Half joke, they want to play once more
Their simple, never-failing game.

So, down their picnic haversack
Goes, and they pile their clothes above.
Then, one shape white and one shape black,
Join at the bright wide open gate
That takes them in and leads them straight
Back to themselves and true hard love.

The mirror rings them, sunned, nude.
And that *piano nobile*
Turns bell-like with their plenitude;
Ringing out, two bare people can
Turn everything Mozartian ...
Or could do, were it not for the

Disaster? One spontaneous
One careless, jubilant gesture, should
That send that carillon through that house?
They knocked the mirror. In a crash
It crumples; crumbles; and one flash
Brings rain in shattered glass and wood.

The darkened glass, the whitened strut.
Dust on the floor, fine speck by speck.
They thought themselves alone there, but
Another living thing, the worm
Was close, was close. It too can squirm
In a dark place, and caused this wreck.

What wreck? They stare across the floor,
They pause ... they laugh ... and then go on,
Ringing and singing as before
But ringing out that they mistook,
Love need not, almost cannot look
At its transparent union.

Exercise

Button up warm overcoat, dear polyphone, best
    aptitude,
Safety-pin clasp bucklebrooch, for the downland round
    the bay;
Gambado the frosty downland, on the left hand, on the
    rectitude,
And bedizen the locality, I'll be Harlequin for today.

The whimbrel and the dotterel shall envy such hilarity,
The dead stands of alkanet all carillon us away,
By helleborine and brown bittervetch now farrago our
    congeries
Count me applejohn, count me natterjack, I'll be
    Jackanory today.

Kiss kiss now higglepiggledy, be reciprocal
    topsyturvywise,
First the bombardon, then the piccolo, let the best
    music play;
I'm columniform, be entableture, and around your
    triforium,
Smooth tropical hyperborean, let me fingertip for
    today.

I'll be dragoman, I'll be fugleman, trig womankind,
    doxology,
So riddle me, cassowary-bird, conundrum us every
    way;

Precious monogam, sing our cryptogram, let the
    long-face, po-countenance
Legless mulligrubs of the valley-folk be exterminate
    for a day.

To lavolta in your proscenium, unbuttoning warm
    overcoat,
To rigadoon the high haystack till we conflagrate all
    the hay,
Only count me frugiverous, jolly orange-girl, roly
    dolly-peg,
Be connubicant, intercoursary, and phlebotomize
    me today.

As we lie here in parallel and we *quodlibet* the
    quotidian
Boustrephedon of our jocundity that we brought with
    us on the way,
Just homologize, anthropophagite, for the sun's far
    past meridian,
Sweet carapace, sweet integument, let me Bobadil
    for today.

If you extricate all the isinglass, monoglutamate,
    good philanthropist,
To leave me oxymoribund, exanimate every way,
 Catachrestically, dear proliferate, if you billycock
    the bright yataghan,
We can cachinnate all the same for that, there's
    enough still for next day.

Yet let me tell you, gentle osculate, as you domicile
   with the walking-stick
Down the long cinder-dark hillslope, through the
   dwindle, through the grey,
To where the dark house stands fireless ... start
   counting, on my finger-tips,
But it's abbreviate, that arithmetic, for people - of
   a day.

So I tried the Dictionary

             ... from (like
wind, star, night, sow
             and the numerals)
the common Aryan stock.
             various roots.
as verb, no true
             past. archaic, as
'an act of kindness'.
             'love-tree': the Judas.
'love-vine': the Dodder.
             the word forms many
compound expressions
             of obvious meaning.
(e.g., 'love-nest':
             the meaning of which
I find not obvious).
             unrelated senses:
a guessing game,
             various pastimes with
cards where the Knave
             or Joker wins,
the Traveller's Joy
             (Clematis Vitalba),
and a score of zero.

Fruit Flavours

I

Granules of black, globed
and cumulus into berry. a shine,
a sheen, darkening
into what is a wine. finger
through the braided hoops,
the horned hooks, and detach
an atom of autumn from the planet.
sail it to the red mouth. it breaks
in a spate of sweetness, welling
the mature flavour, without
cost or waiting. only a chosen
slow reach among the sprays,
with deliberateness
... like another darkness
which fruits in a shatter of light.

II

That was no
ordinary season. the white
grapes I left, densed
and pendent in the yard,
sun singed transparently, green
with a brown of bread-crust. leaves
lay glovewise all over
flagstones but all that
wined on the spray, all
that was steadfast. sun and long
clarity had spoken.
now was the turn of the grape.

Message

Not much of a thing
     and a long time to wait
for a time when, between sleep
     and waking, grey truth will come
sunlit. and if, heavy with sleep, you hear
     the flash of a flute, that will be
not much of a thing, but

a god. that you can say for sure
     if you hear it. or maybe his birds
whistling the return of the world, where we
     have come between him and his creatures: it
is not much of a thing. they have a long
     time to wait, but one of these mornings
his fire will burst on us like music

or near star over water, if you
     consider; and scorch us up like a crust.
that you can say, heavy with
     sleep, for sure ... and to come between
him and his creatures, between waking and
     a long sleep for us, is not much of a thing:
the flute music of a god, and it is silent.

Yes

Let them declare who
stand first and last. You,
you just hush, hearing them; like a tree
waiting for the morning
illumination. Yes,

let them declare
and declare. With the noise of a wind.
but you, just hear and hush. We know
the duty of land and
also sun so

let them.
- but yourself, be as a woodland the sun
clarifies of mist (simple
matters of light and be lit), be an
opening landscape.

Let
us open the landscape. Sounds
pass and are gone, but lands
misty in light expanses, make a world
ready and restored. Just let that stand.

Flower of the Mountain
(for Herbert Read)

I consider
            in this still and stony place
            between sea and mountain
Those who
            at one with the
            rupted, disrupted planet, its
            rent and torrent, quake,
            earthquake, core-tremor,
            tremendous chord of discord,
Those few who
            at the fuse of now, the
            brunt of its
            troubled or flaring frontier
Still
            (as this green jet of a
            seaward country) run
            their springs through deep beds to
Issue gently. The all they do,
Humane and retiring.
            ... fissured into
            a seep of sweetness.
And I
Hardly see this
            appraisal and raising nature as - `
As anti-nature:
            for
            heavy with rightness, authentic,
            ancient in its seeming as the rocks of
            our west, our ledge where

            the wave bursts in greenness, in
            these last and modest pastures,
            is it not the
Second and
Heavenly nature?
            bedrock
            as this archaean
            erode and overthrust
            determining at once the
            angry outcrop and small
Flower of the Mountain?

Seated Within My Orchard

It has gone from me
Which is absurd.

Goodness that can be
Like thrushbill to worm, simple
And final, I have touched it.
Now I have touched it
With age and much talking. Goodness

Like the time of an apple, one fall,
One stroke, there lies goodness on the earth
For the taking: which is absurd.

Spring and autumn springs
And autumns, the land is misted:
The eye is misted. And the apple
Falls to rot alighting. Yes,
Wizening and softening, in flight,
Till the earth has no place for it.

And the worm,
Man is a worm. I do not know
What morning will be black with thrushbill
And final for me, now that goodness has gone
Flashing on its way.

What is left to him?
It has gone on its way.
Which is absurd.

First Poem I

The notes of a tune
Branch into air. Sunlight
Deepening into the room, with time, a little tired,
listening as you sing and play.
But call back what you said.

Let us do it again.
How much is left to us
I do not want to tell you at once or
in the belly of the fish.
So put your hand on my heart.

Life howls in the old dog
at sunrise, and where the road dies
into upland country. The chords grow fuller
and deeper on the other side,
with nightfall early, and raining.

I do not know why
it came to an end
and I put it aside with your hand.
The one that came from the sea,
Her head dripping, enormous,

I had wronged her in nothing.
So it was, for many days, nights,
My tongue was a stone in my mouth.
If I picked my words
Like the raven does bones, to go hungry

54

Was another name for it.
It shall never be built. I do not like
The front of the grey wall from the west, nor
    the stone voice of the sea,
    nor what I see we become,

    having stood in fear of what
    the hero, the clown
and the trembling ass heard the last of
    in a dry valley where the
    silence made them vomit,

    but you have only to think
    it shall not be put to silence
but made much of, and music of - such music
    as shall be for our good
    and never come to harm

    between one day and the next,
    and he shall stay himself, his hand
shall go to the wall - and the wall
    shall be gone. You shall live ...
    he, shall be the same as ever.

First Poem II

A flash above the banks.
Earth brown, and grey water, exalted
Into fire and ocean, terrible to fishes.
The hunter has returned
to feed in the clean water.

What I have to say
is short, and beyond belief; but
few shall be at the trouble of it.
Thus it is with purity:
it is swift, terrible, and

clean as a kingfisher.
The snow and willow-wood
barn owl must wrench, tug,
to take off a mouse's head; my
hand is yours for the asking

in the grief of another morning
flash as the busy mole
of night-time sun, like a kingfisher
(my fish) bursts on our
lake, which is of sleep, nearness

and ageing. When we touch
let that be swift, terrible
and holy too, as is the nature of the world
when it has come to itself
and everything shall be different.

A burn the breadth of a nation
   you can have any minute,
leaving some moles, cave-bats, many monsters,
   movement along the Main Sequence
   a great way, then restitution

   out of four first things,
   like coal ... in water ... and inert
part of the air, they would breed again,
   without hurry or sex;
   but holiness does not burn.

   The lion's roaring, that shall come too late
   for the hunter, the cloud of smoke
and falling tree, and all the juices of the body,
let them be as if they were not ...
   other than the pure stream

   that came to us dreaming,
   but we awoke, and it stood before us,
redeeming the dust of the ground, and streams'
   trickle, into fire and ocean
   that shall be yours for the asking ...

   Holy One.

Sea-Bell Music

Heed the bell's remote note
    For a moment, the clang over broken water
With the friends distant. Bight and swell
    To arrange the scene, broken without
        The measurement of voices'

Disorder yet, like a stroke of the bell
    Into perfection falling momentarily
And seldom. Heed remote islands
    Below skylines, where I went
        in the healing boat

To think out what I could do: friends
    Distant, the scene broken and
The reiterating bell, like the boat's
    Little blizzard at the bows, dividing light
        Not of intent but

In the nature of the case, into dazzle
    And question. Clang. Overfall
Oversewn with sun. For a moment, bell
    Clang, water's race and rip,
        Friends distant

From all these lank, sheer-water islands
    (Where blade edge of bell's
Breaking note on broken water
    Arranged the scene) arranged the scene
        Perfect and seldom.

Landfall

In the hour of littleness, and without
    hope of a clean arrival, clear
as a chime, let the seekers
    consider who the giver may be. in the hour of

weariness from the soiling
    and unwashable, let the takers
consider the sources of strength and
    that a man may stand above dirt

though dirty by a simple
    expedient: and that in
the hour of the self, the
    giver and taker, great

as the earth. seekers for the hour of
    the great arrival, the ship
long brine-washed, as it glides
    cleanly by the chime-strewn meadows, what is it
                       seeking

but to be soiled again? all
    things in their place, the sources of strength,
                  striking
    the rich hour, at the harbour?

Winner and Loser

Where light as heavy as rock
    Rises from the rock
At white midday, the time
    Has come to know
Ourselves and the passing of time

Calmly as the moon and bright
    Jupiter that arc
Together over the vast
    Middle of the Galaxy
They darken with their light

Until fiery day's
    Light, lit fingers
Send them below the mountain:
    Look, which is winner, which
Loser, who shall decide?

So, the fine gold we win
    Skin-deep in sunlight,
Shall we win or lose it back
    That black day we enter
The hillside's stony patience?

For the Daughters of the Earth and Sea

I

      Creatures like rocks but
      Open-handed, and aloof as
the wild swan, but like rocks,
this is the last place,
with the sea's footed foam and
a few stars and stones you old women
      stir as you mumble about
  blindness, while something alive seems to
        hover among you
      like a jewel in the fingers of crones ...

      ... but mounted, in a flash turns
      to a waterfall of blackness;
   open-handed, I have nothing to say,
   arriving at sea, at dawn,
to hush and listen, let it be heavy news
      you will spare a bountiful minute
from your million winters unmoving between
      your father and mother
   embraced, to have to speak to

   no one but yourselves. And
      to be ageless can mean
  two very different things. Like
  to rest among stones, or stars:
or to gaze at the world or end of the world. Holding
      to such a moment of arrival

by a dark shore, in a gathering light
    showing limbs
of women to be different from stones.

    When my eyes rest on
      your bodies that morning
  holds and beholds, I see no
  passage of time, only
(when the time for words has passed) I peer and
                              glimpse
    simple unfamiliar things like
the fell and the dire. To which your crocus
    dress fit to lie with
  any man, does not allure me.

    Unseeing ones I think I
    have seen, see where something
lies between us: a question
of vision I can envisage
without help of your watery diamond: perceiving
    perception is almost enough
by this terrible calm sea: coming to
    see how, flower-like
  resolve needs no resolution.

    Concede me something of
    wisdom, selecting for
silence, it is shown for folly: to be
unconcerned is sufficient. Understand

nothing to be understood, sea-and-earth daughters
        where with light I have come to
    the usual way: the way right for
            a usual man when
        the time for words has passed.

II

            Sea-choruses, they sound
            loud in the ear. Loud
        in the air. I have not come
        like a hero, with the hand of a thief
            snatching at the eye.
            I have come like a man.

            Your parts of the world
            strike cold on my body. Cold
        also, and terrible, your choruses.
        Hesiod wrote about you.
            One of you well-clad,
            one in yellow,

            and it may be, what he meant
            was the heath I came by and
        this burn of gold sand. Then
        sea makes always a third ...
            indivisible.
            But I do not give credit to

      demythologizing
      a hostile environment. I
have not come for that, and shall
call things by their names.
      You shall hear what I think it.
      I think it holiness.

      The truth is, holiness
      is in the sea, the land,
the air, much closer than womb
and woman. But I must tell you, I happen
      also to believe it
      music and Muse now

      in the dim of the morning
      by the sea's din. So that
everything shall be given back, to
you, you goddesses, the word
      named, embodied:
      goddesses.

III

So, We, the Daughters, we have seats by the sea,
      and we have nothing
      ... to lose or to gain.
      The indivisible is a friend
      ... of the poor. We,

without money or children or fire, but with endless
        time, reflect
        on the Last and the All
    but modestly. You could say, like Cobblers.
        Look down, our feet

are the feet of creatures, because from the start we
                                            belong
        with the shore horses'
        plunging roaring. So
    we suffer ... we suffer it gladly.
        And within us, life

flushes to a flash of seeing after blindness.
        What stranger
        looking for wisdom
    or trouble, can fail to see
        the way our step

is light ... yes, look, there is light in our step!
        If you approach us
        like women or gods,
    we shall show, shall show ...
        ... willing as ever.

IV

Now, in the last place,
those who come from there,
where the sea speaks,
and bring the harvest of it, what they bring
cannot be of the earth.
So we cannot think it
less than heavenly.

If you have been in terror, you
can put your hands down
and pick up the dew, to wash with.
When light takes over the morning, for those
turning inland, and climbing
with a glance shoulderward,
rocks on that strand

show human but ageless,
which is the nature of a god.
When sea's indivisible
influence, mounting like raincloud or angels
flows landward
(falling inland woods
soak, drench, drip)

everything dissolves: in time.
A usual thing to say.
But this great space, and light,

and when that is over, this darkness, great silence,
    we have an eye for them. In time
    the end of the world is achieved.
    Such is its resolution.

V

... and She who in her body showed the signs of life,
her straddled core carrying the brown lamb-badge
of birth, I am blest if I know what to call it, as she
stepped, big-limbed, and open-handed, from the sea,
you would not have recognized the earth.

Not have recognized the earth intact without her.

Structure to 'Done'

consider their joy.

there is nothing like it
on the ball of the world.
after-roll and aftermath,
a cockboat shall sail them.

let the birds and beasts
surround us like a wall.
if they pray, it will turn to water.

let rain thunder on the roof,
delight shall never leave them.
it never left them.

the mordacious tick
of the clock shall be music; and what is more,
the tick-bird shall graze, slyboots,
where you never thought of.
here is the clew before her,
leading to our heart of hearts.

if we rode that ride
all day it would never be over,
being innate, being in the nature
of animals such as ourselves

and it is matchless

so rejoice, rejoice, delight
has come to hand, rag-bolt it
to the time of day, pay it in,
over-handed, your marvellous goodness,
this is what we have done.

Structure to 'Found'

let them be without word
of time or place for it, until
it stands before us, gravely:

you will be at a great distance,
will not have news of its coming,
but so swiftly, so fearfully,
they shall be weak with fear.

you could steel yourself,
but the speed of the sun and the moon
is not slow. what is the good
of what cannot be true? all we have is

to speak hurried words, a few of them, and
turn our backs, and go.

dear good land

the underbreath of the wind
is too light for the ear.

it is long since they listened or spoke, and now
it is not to be found.

Cone Poem

Read me the bit
again about the thing
that is pure. I shall not hear
so many words, goodness
shall globe and arise: marvellous
glimmering cone of the zodiac
light against

impossible odds.
Meaning as a cone of light.
Light! The main sequence
we cannot turn our eyes to.
You begin it.

What we have lost,
good friend, reading
over and over again
against impossible odds
in the failing light (light!
it has almost gone from the earth)
you begin it.

Slack Water

Close your book, look up reader, and outside
  see if the sea is quickening, sharp
of the flood tide in outcome and inroad
  moving with the moon toward the land: but

let the easy pulse and heart's blood stream
  truth meteor-bright, its message is
what I hope I shall not say
  in code or clear until dust pays for all

or nothing. The old thoughts run
  like stitches, my pocket is holed, head aches
with what it knows. They say the quiet-voiced
  ebb races fiercest (green buoy for wreck)

and if the man or main theme, octaved and imperial
  return in the major for you, still my head and hand
are void and devoid; till, if words will not come
  to tongue or pen for what is right in stone

have it so: or if the living and the dead
  reverse their roles, you see how it is; for all
I care now (let them have their say) I say
  let pin or penny drop, reader, have it so.

Stone Poem

I was in your hands.
Greatnesses and goodnesses, we were not
            at home with them,
because of our needs: black struts
    of wrecks, proud out of ebb
            no doubt, we
    cut no better figure; nor
            you may see, now.

The drift of the arch
was fell for us. While we awaited
            the imperial
rescript, engrossed in a curial that never
    preferred us, we were left
            to purge our
    contempt: limb of the sun
            lion-like on sea-limb.

Once, if you took
your clothes off, one half the world
            fell dark. Now,
the dry dustmouse, under the bed
    takes pride of place; and I gravely
            fear
    my shadow. Let it, though,
            take its time, for

        if we played sun-
and planet-wheel, in those years (and you
            tell me

which of us was which), stuffed lion
        or doll-pig now, because of our
                needs, of your
        greatnesses and goodnesses must ... *faugh,*
        Am I God?

        The wind being up,
veer more rope, to be ready; but
                in the dead
port only my head swims.   Whichever of us,
        runagate and uncomely, fled,
                loser,
        loser pays for all, tomb and tombstone.
                Nihil obstat.

Westerly

Winds, they are of the sun's making, I suppose,
  and so is time, in which they change.
You do not see how they change, but I
  do not understand it merely;

I also fear. Yet, for them to be joyful
  all summer was easy, and I believe
swell and weathered stormcone will not change that.
    You
  believe what you can. In such a westerly

as this, steel windows drone and whistle
  as much as the other kind. I know
that from the one beside me; but you cannot,
  until your house is of glass,

know what tower over me and never speak
  save when this window screams into my book:
once, my hands were soiled with their mouths
  that now, deeply, the earth quenches. Now also

whatever soils hands, keep to yourself. Those,
  sure woodenly to outlast the planter, would not
be able to breathe it, were it only the
  late blackberries (so ripe, there was no taste in them)

dewy with autumn storm, that took away
  one of my thirsts, when leaves' bletting and branding
first blared winter. As for the other, let it
  rage or end; but then, if the end is in sight,

think of me: I am blind, as I was
   before it all began; and there are things
I cannot do, even if I try, which you
   also must take on trust. I have found it hard, but

truly it is vouched for by now. Those fountains
   more light than water, leave them to do
for us, what they cannot but do: which you must know
   before I tell you, on this planet of winds.